Personal is Political

by
Liam Whear, Penny Gotch &
Susan Wright

Copyright

Dedication

To the protestors in Ferguson, Mexico, Hong Kong, Palestine, and everyone else fighting for liberation.

Table of Contents

"Born Slippy"

by Liam Whear

Upppppppppppppppppppp. Thrown in and you hope it matters. You are carried across seas of arms, one in hundreds, hundreds in one.

The year is 1995. You're surrounded by hundreds of sweaty people, dancing, living. A warehouse in South London, and this is where you want to spend your life. The Second Summer of Love went and now it's just about the dirt, and the catharsis.

No one should stop you.

The hordes of people crashing round you become one, and you are with them. Go with the beat. You remember the Criminal Justice Act. How they thought they could stop you. You can feel the peak inside you, and the full force of everything you love. When you feel this strong, you should use what you know to be the change you want to see.

The deep bass follows your every move. There is something here, in these dank walls and among these throbbing people. It's remarkable because, before, there wasn't. Before it was empty. But that's what you liked. Celebrated the nothingness, filled it with all you could and didn't think twice.

In this moment, now, it matters though. You thrash out, hundreds of bodies fling against you. All in solidarity. What was once boorish aggression, becomes force. As the rush comes, you are lifted.

Be part of a movement. Happiness is not a crime. Happiness is not a danger. Happiness should be free.

The peak is here. Whatever you are, is now everything. Or nothing. Whatever. Weightlessness. Everything you've loved has always been here, it's just time to know how to fight for it. But that can wait for now. Right now, love yourself. And others. Spread enlightenment. Risk everything. Because it's damn worth it. Trust me.

You are not a crime.
You are alive.
Go.

"The Lights Go Out"

by Penny Gotch

Out at the pub. The rumble of voices and the clink of glasses. The sweet-sour smell of cider and its sparkle on your laughing tongue.

Just a regular Saturday night out with uni friends, or so you think.

You won't remember this part. But you will remember later.

You're merry. You're having fun. Nothing can touch you and everything is right with the world.

Time slips past you like oiled silk and you barely notice until you check your phone.

It's ten minutes to twelve. You live twenty minutes away.

And at midnight, the street lights go out.

You make your excuses. Plead tiredness, work in the morning, anything that will let you go now. You have to make it home and you can't afford a cab.

Out onto the street. The pavement is wet and glistening like the hide of a slug. You stagger along in your heels, wishing you'd gone for flats instead.

Everything is quiet except for the rhythmic tap of your footsteps.

You're going to make it. You've got to.

The buildings around you lean down to inspect you. Not threatening, but confused, like old men wondering over the child scurrying along below them.

You're half way there.

The lights go out.

Two hours from now, you'll be sitting at the bottom of your shower with the heat up as high as you can stand. And you'll scrub at your skin until it almost bleeds and fight back the choking sobs.

Two weeks from now you'll make a report and the questions will start.

"What were you wearing? Were you drunk? Were you walking home alone? Why would you go home after dark?"

You'll go to the doctor. You'll get on pills for anxiety. You won't tell anybody why.

Two months from now, you'll find a support group online and they'll give you strength and hope.

You'll start looking into street lights and the safety of being seen. You'll scour the Internet, research, learn and study.

You'll get angry.

Two years from now, you'll marvel at the way that an egg fits perfectly in the palm of your right hand. Then you'll draw back your arm and lob that egg at a politician's face.

It'll hit him square in the jaw and he'll recoil in surprise and pain, dripping yellow. You'll punch the air in celebration in the brief moment between attack and the response from security.

They'll hit you with pepper spray and put you in cuffs. But to you, it's worth it.

But that's all to come. Right now, you're alone in the streets.

And the lights have gone out.

You pull out your phone to light your way, walking slowly. If you just stay calm, you can make it home safe.

Somebody grabs your wrists and pulls. You can't fight, not in heels, but you scream anyway.

Nobody comes.

He wrenches the phone out of your hand and throws it away. The battery pops out and the screen cracks.

The lights go out.

"Feminism Misunderstood"

by Susan Wright

Have years of mixed standpoints confused the masses?

Contemporary feminism came about in an explosion of radical demand. Which, contrary to general belief, stemmed from the actions of 'mere' housewives. A people whose desire was for life to reach outside of the home. This approach was void of any association with racism or classism.

Essentially, women wanted access to all the opportunities open to men. From this, the feminism campaign has since expanded its fences to tackle more and more life situations in which women are plighted by sexism.

In the not-so-distant-past we have seen women's rights override stereotypical living, seen new laws written and have been heard by the masses. However, there is work yet to be done. And without a fixed objective to umbrella feminism under, people are confused. We ask ourselves, *'am I a feminist? If I am, does that make me a man-hater? If I'm not, does that make me a misogynist?'*

Amid our social climate, men and women are unsure when defining feminism alongside their personal ideals. Ultimately, feminism is a call for freedom of gender-related judgements. After all, what does a person's body have to do with their aptitude at life?

Somehow, feminism has been interpreted as a pro-women and anti-men organisation. The assumption is thinking that feminism serves to gain dominance over men. In reality, equal rights mean fair opportunities for both sexes. And the current imbalance of power needs to be equalised, not taken over.

Emma Watson, UN Women Goodwill Ambassador, addressed just that in her 2014 speech, which introduced the HeForShe campaign. Watson formerly extended an invitation for all men to support gender equality. Her statement, "*gender equality is your issue too*", was the resounding message.

Shockingly the 2014 WomenAgainstFeminism campaign is one example of the misinformed views of feminism. We witnessed groups of young girls posting memes that discredited feminism as an excuse for women to parade themselves as victims and misandrists. While their obvious naivety is laughable (and in retaliation many posted their arguments for why they *do* need feminism), it does fortify the importance of clarifying what feminism is.

Wonderful as it is for those who feel they have never been discriminated against, that does not stand as reason enough to assume everyone has the same experience. It is becoming a common argument that feminism is no longer needed but it is not based on an understanding of all women's lives except a very egoistic perspective. The term intersectionality, coined by Kimberlé Crenshaw in 1989, is :

"The view that women experience oppression in varying configurations and in varying degrees of intensity. Cultural patterns of oppression are not only interrelated, but are bound together and influenced by the intersectional systems of

society. Examples of this include race, gender, class, ability, and ethnicity".

Intersectionality is now another element of feminism, which voices the differing degrees of suffering.

From study figures released by the *World Health Organisation,* in eastern countries almost 60% of women killed, are spouse victims. Likewise, of women murdered in England, Wales and the US, over 40% are at the hands of their partner.

"Compared with 6.3% of murders of men by spouse [in high-earning countries and 3.6% in low-earning countries. These] results underscore that women are disproportionately vulnerable to violence and murder" – Dr. Heidi Stöckl.

They also show that figures differ between regions and even so, from extreme domestic violence to equality in pay, women are vulnerable all across the world.

In 2014, *The Independent* reported the UK's drop from being one of the 20 most gender-equal countries. "*Women are [still] earning only three-quarters, 77%, of what men in full-time comparable jobs earn.*"

How is it possible that more than four decades after the Equal Pay Act women are still subject to lowered salaries?

Physical abuse is beyond appalling compared to getting a smaller paycheque but what we are actually seeing is that sexism is routed in major establishments. Places where they should be the pinnacle example of gender-equality. But are not.

Sexism is still at the heart of our society and we need feminism to eradicate it.

If you believe in the fair treatment of all people, regardless of gender, next time you wonder if you're a feminist, feel assured that the answer is yes.

Molly Penford's Art: Part One

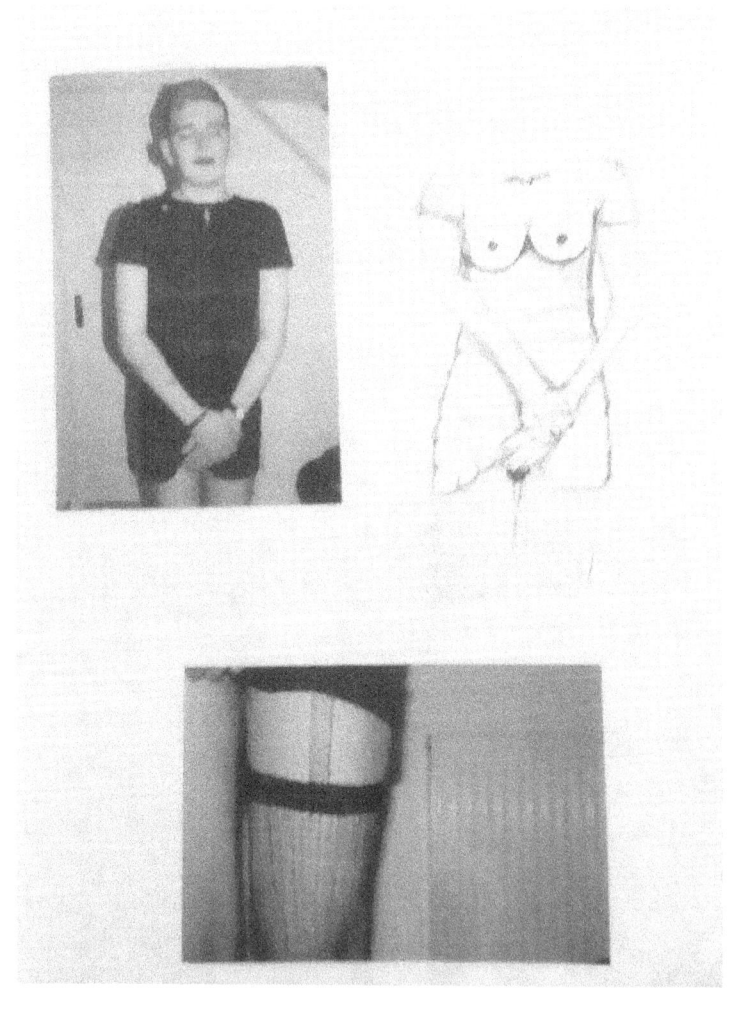

"The Desire Begins with the Demand to Live Not as an Object But as a Subject of History... (Greil Marcus)"

by Liam Whear

"The desire begins with the demand to live not as an object but as a subject of history – to live as if something actually depended on one's actions – and that demand opens onto a free street."

– Greil Marcus, 1989

Coating my fingernails in black, it feels like I'm preparing for something. I want people to look at me differently, not because I am, but because it's what I want. I want to look glamorous because I want to feel glamorous. I want to look defiant because I want to feel defiant. I want to look strong because I want to feel strong.

Our bodies aren't just temples. Our bodies are real and tangible. They can hurt. And they can shine bright. Because my body is the most immediate part about me, I make it represent me. I wear punk patches and badges. I shave my hair and wear piercings. I project my fantasies onto myself.

Existence is a statement itself. Every new day is a new day of being alive. It's trite but it's true. It's an idea of decoration, and progress. We equate progress with change.

There's probably a reason I still call it "dressing up". Internalised masculinity? For it is my true self. And therefore, in my own fucked up way of looking at it, something to be earned. I can't explain it either. But it makes me excited and sad at the same time. As someone who lives off experiences, I need to be my *own* experience. To stand. I is I.

People know who I am. Everything is connected. I see my life as a statement because it revolves around my fucked up queer friends and seeking experiences with them. I'll die with them.

"Eating While Fat"

by Penny Gotch

I'm fat.

Stop right there. I know what you're going to say.

"You're not fat! You look fine!"

As well-intentioned as those words are, they aren't true.

Fat is not a bad word. It's an adjective and a noun. It explains how I look. It is an element of my being. And that is not an inherently bad thing.

I'm fat. And I'm okay with that.

Well. Most of the time.

So let's take it as read that I am what I say I am. I'm a fat person.

And as a fat person, living itself is an act of bravery.

Society judges fat. And society hates fat.

Fat is lazy. Fat is greedy. Fat is ugly. Fat is an all-powerful insult and judgement.

Just living as a fat person in our fatphobic society is a scary, oppressive experience.

But there are two activities that a fat person can undertake in public that render us supremely vulnerable.

The first one is exercise.

You see, there's a terrible catch-22 with fatness and fitness.

A fat person who doesn't exercise is a slob worthy of ridicule. Yet a fat person who is exercising is a figure of fun fit for verbal abuse.

Try to figure that one out. No matter what we do, we're mocked.

Now the exercise issue isn't such a problem for me.

I prefer getting my physical for practical reasons over exercising for its own sake. You won't catch me jogging when I could be walking to the shops for groceries instead.

But there is another public activity. One that does concern me. Another action just as radical as exercising while fat. A simple biological function that everyone must perform to survive.

Eating.

If you are fat, consuming anything edible in public becomes a horrible, stressful experience.

It could be something as "healthy" as an apple. Or it could be something as "unhealthy" as a chocolate bar.

It doesn't matter.

If you're fat and you're eating, people will assume that you shouldn't be.

After all, you're fat. You don't need those calories, do you? Of course you don't.

I haven't received harassment for eating in public. Not yet. But it's something that I fear.

If I buy a sandwich for lunch and walk down the street eating it, I can feel people watching me.

I see the way that people look at me. A fat person filling her face.

Maybe I'm paranoid. Maybe I'm not. But if you search online for long enough, you'll find stories of people hearing the words "You shouldn't be eating that".

And that is why I rebel.

I refuse to let the potential judgement of

bigots force me to change my behaviour.

They may think I should eat nothing but lettuce in public. Or better yet, nothing at all.

I don't care.

Whether it's fruit, a pork pie or even a full meal from McDonalds, I know what my body needs and I will provide it.

I will eat while fat. Deal with it.

"Our Ruin"

by Susan Wright

Jeremiah 2:7 - I brought you into a fertile land to eat its fruit and rich produce. But you came and defiled my land and made my inheritance detestable.

We strip our planet of its resources. Logging, mining and now fracking. Our industries pollute. Our one-crop farms, fertilizers, insecticides poison. And snobbery rejects 'ugly' fruit. We are capable of living greener lives. Yet, we do not. And our energy is put into building nuclear power stations instead of wind farms.

It is not normal that people feign a state of disbelief or disinterest when issues of environment are raised. That these same irresponsible people raise children in their damaging habits. That these children's children, along with ours, will be left to resurrect a dying planet. That they will likely fail to do. Because, "when the damage is done" … it cannot always be undone.

Molly Penford's Art: Part Two

"Fuck Yr Macho White Boy Entitlement"

by Liam Whear

I don't mean to invest all my energy into what is really an abstract concept, but I do. I've since learned that every idol is a false idol, so for now I'll continue to stick to abstracts.

When did punk rock begin? Who cares? When did punk rock die? *Who cares*?

What punk rock does for me is take everything I know and everything I have experienced and makes them important. It compares, contrasts, and correlates them with everything else. Look in the mirror and say, 'this is valid'. Look in the mirror and say, 'this is fucked'.

When I first listened to the Manic Street Preachers everything started to make sense, and I realised how important this all was to me, and millions of others. It was something to care about. To invest time in. To invest a life in. I guess I do buy into the mythology and romanticism. I'll take that. But it's a form of escapism that roots itself in the real and gives people the energy to do shit.

But I also understand it's not always a safe space. People with idealised notions go in and feel their responsibilities slacken. "I listened to a Clash song once, they weren't racist so I'm not racist". There's that club, 924 Gilman Street, that has "No Racism, No Sexism, No Homophobia" stencilled on the front. Entitled jerks come on and feel that that's that, they've entered Liberal Heaven. And then touch a girl up inside and laugh at a racist joke. The true bastions of our precious liberal Punk Rock.

Punk isn't above diversity. It shouldn't be. It's not a utopia of DIY notions and accepting handshakes, it's made up of real people who do shitty things. Like it or not, it *is* the same subculture that spewed out GG Allin and "iconic" White Power band Skrewdriver. And it is our shared responsibility as punks and punk enthusiasts to bare this burden. Punks don't question because they're "above that". They're not. You're not. I'm not.

Punk musicians and punk fans wear their beliefs on their sleeves (sometimes literally). Punk is (or should be) inherently political by its very nature by its DIY ethos and supposedly "no bullshit" stance. And punk is a consuming lifestyle for many, punks adopting it as their own personal aesthetic.

Punk brought me to life, punk taught me to care, and punk taught me to love. I will still do my best to fight those polluting the scene, and will tell them to fuck off. Because I want to live, I want to care, and I want to love.

"Devil's Advocate"

by Penny Gotch

For you, it's an intellectual debate
about modern society,
its sensitivities.
"Everything is offensive these days."
But you're wrong.
It's being denied a heart transplant
because my neurotype is "broken".
It's sympathy given to the mother
who tried to murder me.
It's the 85% chance of unemployment,
the 4-10 times more likely to be assaulted,
the 90% chance of sexual abuse
in my lifetime.
R*tarded is just a word for you.
For me? It's life or death.

"Car Ride"

by Susan Wright

Did you know, drivers breathe five times more pollution than cyclists? I didn't. Suppose I thought it'd be the other way round, what with people on bikes actually in the fume-riddled traffic, weaving at the backs, sides and fronts of cars. Seems I was wrong. Though, it wouldn't be the first time.

I heard it on the radio. Honestly, I usually listen to Katy Perry or Taylor Swift. Don't laugh; I happen to like their music. But listening to those same CDs on repeat for the umpteenth time, I opted for a change.

And I don't know if this has ever happened to you but I found myself totally hypnotised by the presenter's voice. He could talk about anything and I would listen, and anything happened to be pollution.

He said that sitting in the drivers seat put me directly in line with the exhaust emissions of the motorist in front of me. Their fumes go straight into my body. Great. That's all I need in the morning – a toxic cocktail on the way to work. I should have changed to a different station, not good to start the day worried. The reason I didn't, I put down to mind control, or tiredness. It was early, so either made sense.

So there I was, being lulled into listening to a stranger tell me I was being poisoned on a daily basis. He practically told me my lifespan was made shorter with every breath that I took. Which was shocking. Don't get me wrong, I had thought about pollution and the environment and climate change and global warming, and all those "green" things. I've not lived this long with my head in the clouds. It'd simply skipped my mind that it was actually harming me, and not just making the temperature hotter (because I was all for the sunny weather to stay).

Perhaps I'm ignorant. But I'm not, I'm just busy. So busy, that I get a little scatter-brained now and then. Only yesterday, I'd gotten Alfie ready, thought I had five minutes for a quick fag, just to realise I'd misread the time and we ended up being late. Typical. But that's how it is sometimes, I can't be perfect. Alfie got to nursery safe and I got to work. That's all that really matters.

What can I do about pollution anyway? Firstly, I don't know enough about the science of it. Secondly, I have to drive to get places and thirdly, isn't it already too late?

Molly Penford's Art: Part Three

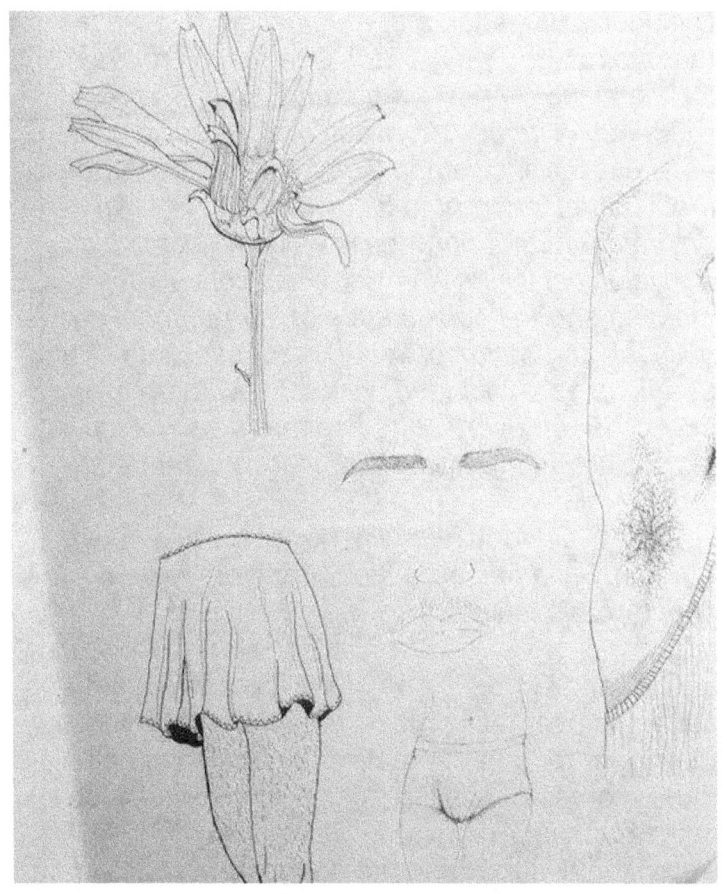

"The Ease of Your Pose"

by Liam Whear

This next piece is an album review of Transgender Dysphoria Blues, *an album released this year by the punk band Against Me!. The reason for its inclusion that frontwoman Laura Jane Grace's existence is immediately put into a political context as she is a transwoman working in an environment that is often ignorant to its own exclusivity. An environment that parades itself on a seemingly mythological inclusivity. Her lyrics convey this melding and the coexistence of the personal and political, and have spoken to a countless amount of people, myself included. When I saw them live (19/11/2014), every song became a validating experience to me and all the fellow queer people around me.*

"Full-body high, I'm never coming down". The body is a battleground. I hope my review conveys this to you.

Laura Jane Grace is one of the most important figures in alternative music today. It's not every day the singer for one of the biggest bands in punk music comes out as transgender in Rolling Stone magazine, but Against Me! were always exceptional, occupying the bridge between mainstream success and the indie borderlines. The 8th of May 2012 was an important day for punk rock as, for a genre that's had its merits muddied in the past with homophobia in the 80s hardcore scene (H.R. of Bad Brains) and transphobia

(Kathleen Hanna of Bikini Kill), it confirmed how far we've come as a scene. Grace, formerly known as Tom Gabel, revealed she had been living with gender dysphoria for most of her life, and had plans to undergo transitioning. And the punk community wholeheartedly embraced Laura for her frankness and bravery.

20 months later, we have *Transgender Dysphoria Blues*. The band's fifth album comes after a series of reissues of their previous work that was perhaps hinting at a radical change in sound. In truth, *Transgender Dysphoria Blues* sits comfortably after *New Wave* and *White Crosses* in its brand of defiant, accessible, loud punk rock sound, but this time it's leaner, brighter and meaner. The majority of the tracks, as suggested via the album title, deal with Grace's experiences as a trans woman, and thus ignite the fire that was burning under the band since they broke through into the mainstream. The songs clearly mean a lot to Grace, and that shines through with conviction.

The band's first two albums, *Reinventing Axl Rose* and *As The Eternal Cowboy*, were special for their youthful energy and the charming messiness of their sound and aesthetic. It's true that Against Me! seems to have fallen in favour of fans of those albums since polishing up their sound, but *Transgender Dysphoria Blues* makes up for it with the songs. "Dead Friend" and the brilliantly titled "FUCKMYLIFE666" offer up strangely haunting melodies while still being uplifting. *"Is your mother proud of your eyelashes / Silicone chest and collagen lips / how can you even recognise me?"* Grace questions atop backing harmonies that brings to mind the best of The

Gaslight Anthem and even The Offspring.

Transgender Dysphoria Blues offers empathy in its tales of self-doubt and hatred. The opening title track sees Grace yelling *"You've got no cunt in your strut, you've got no hips to shake/And you know it's obvious, but we can't choose how we're made"*. Against Me! were always known for combining the personal with the political, and it's excellent to see they still haven't lost what made them special, only making it more potent given the context of this album.

However, all of the alienation and self-hatred is spat back at the listener in the closing of "Black Me Out". *"I don't want to feel that weak and insecure, as if you were my fucking pimp, as if I was your fucking whore"* Grace screams atop thundering drums and guitars. "Black Me Out" is the total catharsis the rest of the album's tracks leads to, and is the most emotional song the band has written in years. Maybe even their best.

Transgender Dysphoria Blues is an album that is going to mean a lot to many of the people who choose to embrace it. Its songs are empathetic to the struggles many LGBTQ people face daily; these songs can become their best friend. *Transgender Dysphoria Blues* is an important album as a bold statement of inner rage and confusion, rallying against dysphoria and judgement. It's also the band's best.

"A Heaven in a Hell"

by Penny Gotch

What is a heaven in a hell?

Going to a concert when autistic.

Yes, autistics go to concerts. I've been to three this year alone.

But it's an experience with both good and bad elements. And not necessarily for the reason you're thinking of.

You see, one aspect of autism that nobody seems to talk about outside the autistic community is sensory processing.

And yet sensory processing problems are incredibly common amongst autistics. Almost universal, I'd say.

Of course, no two autistics are the same. Each one of us has our own individual response to any given stimuli.

But broadly speaking, we have two basic categories: either hypersensitive or hyposensitive.

A hypersensitive autistic lives in a world with everything turned up to eleven. Gentle touches burn the skin, moderate light can blind, and loud sounds are physically painful.

A hyposensitive autistic is the opposite: their world is on mute. Weighted blankets are a relief, strong flavours a necessity, and bright colours soothing.

And it's not uncommon for any given autistic to experience both depending on the sense in question.

For example, it's possible to be

hypersensitive to sight, smell and taste and hyposensitive to sound and touch.

And this isn't even mentioning the non-traditional sense like balance, temperature or pain. Autism can mess around with every single one.

Me? I tend towards the hypersensitive end of the scale for pretty much everything.

And most of the time, it's not a problem. I make adjustments for my issues in every day life.

I cut the labels out of clothes. I wear sunglasses when it isn't particularly sunny. I always have my music with me in case sounds get too much. That sort of thing.

So how is this relevant to concerts?

Simple: they're a sensory atom bomb going off in my face.

First, there are crowds. People push up against each other without meaning to. People brush against you. And if you're hypersensitive to touch, like I am, it feels awful.

And you're standing on your feet for several hours straight. Nowhere to sit down. No relief. That's bad enough when you aren't hypersensitive to pain. Surprise! I am.

Then there's the temperature. The ability to perceive external temperatures and regulate your body temperature? That's a sense too. And concerts get hot.

And don't forget bright lights and visual effects. Those do wonders on hypersensitive sight.

So if there are so many unpleasant aspects, why do I go?

The sound.

I'm hypersensitive to sound. But when it comes to music, it's a blessing, not a curse.

When I'm at a concert, everything in the world seems to melt away.

I close my eyes. My hands move in the air along with what I can hear. And it almost feels like a religious experience.

And that's why I put up with the sensory hell of concerts. Because when you get right down to it, there is nothing on Earth quite like that feeling.

And I wouldn't give it up for the world.

About the Authors: Liam Whear

Liam Whear is a glam punk princess who waxes lyrical about music when they're not being pretty. Nearly a graduate from Canterbury Christchurch University, they mix the overwhelming gazing-into-the-void that entails with writing pieces for Hitsville UK and now Forgotten Pop. They have been published on HerCampus, had prose published in a CCCU anthology (2012, collab with Lampyridae Press) and in an online university magazine (2013, ISSUU).

Their current project is a collection of essays creating a discourse about social and political context amongst music movements and scenes.

Liam lives in Maidstone, Kent, and also likes dogs, Renaissance art and the film *The Room*.

- **Writing blog:
  http://speculationsxx.tumblr.com**
- **Facebook:
  https://www.facebook.com/basedkanye**
- **E-mail: liam_whear@hotmail.com**

About the Authors: Penny Gotch

Penny Gotch is an Essex girl exported to Kent. Writing-wise, she dabbles in most things. Flash fiction? Opinion pieces? Young adult novels? Radio plays, short stories, book and music reviews?

You name it: she does it.

She also does a good copy edit and knows a thing or two about digital marketing. Just saying.

When Penny isn't writing, working or sleeping, her personal interests are as eclectic as her writing, and they run the gamut from professional wrestling to music to baking.

If you want to get to know Penny better, you can e-mail her at pennygotch@gmail.com, check out her website at www.pennygotch.co.uk, or visit her one of her social media pages:

- **Facebook: pennygotchwriter**
- **Twitter/Instagram/Pinterest: pennygotch**
- **Tumblr: pennygotch / pennygotchpoetry**

About the Authors: Susan Wright

Susan Wright is an undergraduate at Canterbury Christ Church University. *Personal Is Political* will be her first published work. Susan lives in Kent and rightly so, as it is her favourite county.

Alongside her love for writing, Susan is an avid reader, a closet painter, and interested in all things personal and political.

About the Artist: Molly Penford

Molly Penford is an art enthusiast with a passion for writing who studies English & Creative Writing at University of Cumbria. She enjoys writing fiction about the wonderful parallel universe she'd like to live in. Whilst not watching documentaries and listening to queer punk, she enjoys drawing landscapes and walking in them.

She is currently working on an essay about women's roles in The Great Gatsby, as well as her portfolio of short stories.

Her dream is to write her own hugely successful graphic novel that she illustrates as well.

Molly lives in Nottinghamshire, and regularly visits art galleries and local gigs. She lives at home in the holiday with her five cats.

She has a photography blog over at http://madasei.tumblr.com

www.ingramcontent.com/pod-product-compliance
Lightning Source LLC
Chambersburg PA
CBHW060341290526
45793CB00003B/691